W9-DGG-562

ILAN RAMON
ISRAEL'S FIRST ASTRONAUT

by Tanya Lee Stone

The Millbrook Press
Brookfield, Connecticut

In memory of the seven heroes
whose lives were lost aboard *Columbia*.

And for Ilan Ramon's wife, Rona,
and their children—Assaf, Tal, Yiftah, and Noa.
—Tanya Lee Stone

Book design by Edie Weinberg and Cezanne Studios.
Front cover photographs courtesy of AP/Wide World Photos.
Back cover photograph courtesy of ©AFP/Corbis.
Photographs courtesy of AP/Wide World Photos: pp. 3, 4-5 (Tyler Morning Telegraph, Dr. Scott Lieberman), 13, 18, 23, 24, 27 (bottom), 29, 33, 34, 36, 39, 40, 42; NASA: pp. 6, 16 (top), 17 (bottom), 20 (top), 21 (bottom), 31, 32, 35, 38; Getty Images: pp. 8 (© Biton Hayel Avir), 11 (© Biton Hayel Avir), 22 (both); © AFP/Corbis: pp. 15, 25

Library of Congress Cataloging-in-Publication Data

Stone, Tanya Lee.
Ilan Ramon, Israel's first astronaut / Tanya Lee Stone.
        p. cm.
Summary: A biography of Israeli astronaut Ilan Ramon, who died in the explosion of the space shuttle Columbia on February 1, 2003.
Includes bibliographical references and index.
ISBN 0-7613-2888-2 (lib. bdg.) — ISBN 0-7613-2376-7 (pbk.)
1. Ramon, Ilan, 1955-2003–Juvenile literature. 2. Astronauts–Israel–Biography–Juvenile literature. 3. Columbia (Spacecraft)–Accidents–Juvenile literature. [1. Ramon, Ilan, 1955-2003. 2. Astronauts. 3. Columbia (Spacecraft)–Accidents.] I.Title.
 TL789.58.R36S76 2003
 629.45'0092–dc21

                              2003009254

Published by The Millbrook Press, Inc.
2 Old New Milford Road
Brookfield, Connecticut 06804

"12 . . . 11 . . . 10 . . . 9 . . . 8 . . .
We have a go for main engine start,
5 . . . 4 . . . 3 . . . 2 . . . 1 . . .
Booster ignition . . . and liftoff of
the space shuttle
Columbia . . ."

It was 10:39 on the morning of January 16, 2003. A crowd of people had gathered as they always do when a liftoff is scheduled. The crowd heard the roar and saw *Columbia* blast off–up, up, up into the clear blue sky. It was not *Columbia's* first launch. The National Aeronautics and Space Administration (NASA) had used *Columbia* for twenty-two years. It had traveled into space twenty-seven times before. The people on the ground cheered as the spacecraft climbed higher and higher toward space.

The mighty *Columbia* spent the next sixteen days in space. Everything went smoothly. All systems were "go." Science experiments were carried out. The crew members had fun as they worked. They listened to music, sent e-mail messages from space to Earth, and kept the world up to date on their mission.

A large crowd gathered again on February 1, 2003. It was a warm, sunny day. This time people were waiting to welcome the crew safely home. Everyone was excited. *Columbia* was heading back to Earth right on schedule. Then, at 8:52 A.M., just a few minutes before *Columbia* was to touch down, a problem was noticed. Ground control in the operations room at NASA was watching the computers. They could see that temperatures had started to rise in the brakes, wheels, and wing flaps. By 8:59 A.M. none of the sensors were working. Ground control radioed the shuttle crew about the problem. Shuttle commander Rick Husband said, "Roger, uh . . ."

Those were the last words anyone ever heard from the crew of *Columbia*. At 9:00 A.M. all communication was lost. Bright flashes and loud booms quickly followed the silence. People in Texas, Louisiana, and Arkansas saw the shuttle blasting apart. Many held out hope that the astronauts would be okay. But there was little chance of happy news. At 2:04 P.M.. President George Bush told the world, "The *Columbia* is lost; there are no survivors."

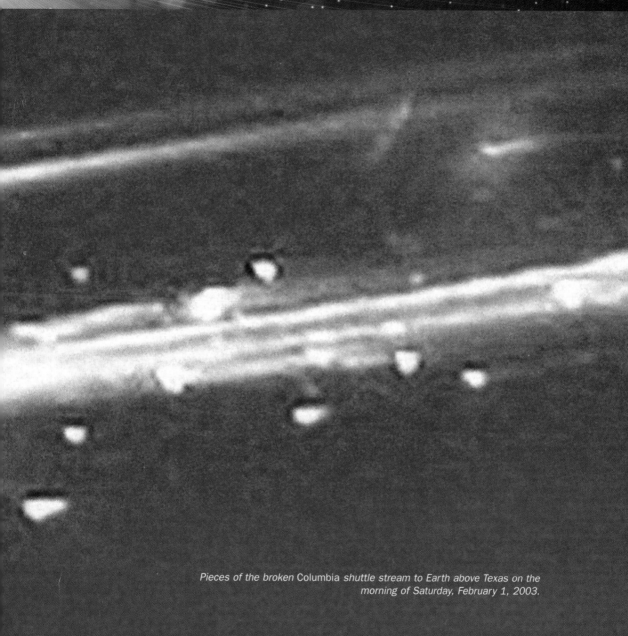

Pieces of the broken Columbia shuttle stream to Earth above Texas on the morning of Saturday, February 1, 2003.

The world lost seven astronauts that day. Six of them—Rick Husband, William McCool, Michael Anderson, Kalpana Chawla, David Brown, and Laurel Clark—were American. One of them, Ilan Ramon, was the first person from the country of Israel to travel into space. This is his story.

In the Beginning

On June 20, 1954, Ilan was born in a small city called Ramat Gan near Tel Aviv, Israel. His birth name was Ilan Wolferman. Ilan grew up in the Israeli cities of Ramat Gan and Beersheba. He and his older brother, Gadi, were born in Israel but their parents were not.

Ilan's father is Eliezer Wolferman. He was born in Germany. Many Jewish people left Germany and other parts of Europe in the years just before World War II. They were being treated badly and were afraid things would get worse. The Wolfermans left Germany in 1935. Eliezer and his father fought in the war that made Israel an independent nation in 1948.

Tova, Ilan's mother, was born in Poland. Tova and her family stayed in Poland during World War II. They suffered at the hands of Adolf Hitler and his Nazi party. More than six million Jews were killed in the Nazi Holocaust. Most of Tova's family members died. Somehow she and her mother stayed alive in Auschwitz, one of the worst Nazi concentration camps. They went to live in Israel in 1949. That is where Tova met and married Eliezer Wolferman.

Top Fighter Pilot

Ilan was the Wolferman's younger son. He was a popular boy and got top grades in school. He was very good at science and math. When Ilan was sixteen, a neighbor took him for a ride in a small plane. Ilan was hooked on flying! He graduated from high school two years later. It was time for him to join the military. Most eighteen-year-old Israeli men and women must serve in the military. No one was surprised when Ilan chose to go to flight school for the Israeli Air Force (IAF). Ilan then fought in the Yom Kippur War. This was a war with Egypt and Syria that lasted for three weeks in October 1973.

Flying for the air force was a thrill for Ilan. Sometimes he would meet with his old high school friends in other parts of the military. They would swap stories. One friend, Reuven Segev, remembered an exciting story Ilan told one night. Ilan's steering wheel had gotten stuck, and he and his flight teacher both had to jump out of the plane! Segev said, "There was no eject seat. Ilan had to crawl out onto the tail and jump, like in the movies." He was hurt from the fall and had to stay out of the sky for a few months. But Ilan still graduated first in his class in 1974. He was a top combat fighter pilot.

Ilan with an F-16 behind him. The F-16 Falcons have become one of the most popular fighter jets.

After flight school, Ilan changed his last name. The first prime minister of Israel had done the same thing. Prime Minister David Ben-Gurion felt that the people fighting for Israel should have Hebrew names. He changed his birth name of David Green to David Ben-Gurion to set an example. Ilan followed in his footsteps. He made the name Ramon from some of the letters in Wolferman.

Ramon was a natural pilot. First he flew A-4 aircraft. Then he flew Mirage III-C fighter jets. Then a new fast, light fighter plane called the F-16 was made, beginning in 1978. Several nations wanted them for their air forces. Israel was one of them. The IAF formed an F-16 squadron. Ramon was one of the first pilots chosen. He and his fellow IAF pilots traveled to the United States. They trained at the F-16 Training Course at Hill Air Force Base in Utah.

Ramon went back to Israel after this training. He served in the IAF as the deputy squadron commander-B, F-16 squadron, for the next three years. Then the IAF carried out a surprise mission using eight F-16 planes in June 1981. They sent eight of their best fighter pilots to destroy a nuclear reactor in Iraq. The eight planes flew together in a tight group. This way, radar would not see them as small fighter planes. Instead they looked like one large jet plane.

The youngest pilot chosen for the mission was Ramon. He was only twenty-seven years old. Major General Amos Yadlin flew in the same mission. He said the other pilots called Ramon the Kid. "He was coolheaded, modest, sort of a humble hero—not like most macho top-gun flyers." Ramon fought in Operation Peace for Galilee the next year. This war was fought in Beirut, Lebanon. Both sides fought hard and many were killed. Ramon took a break from the IAF after this war and went to college.

Just back from a daring 1981 mission to destroy a nuclear reactor in Iraq, Ilan Ramon (standing, upper left) and his fellow pilots seem relieved and happy to be safe on the ground. This photograph was provided by the Israeli military, which intentionally blurred the faces of the two men in the second row.

From Student Back to Pilot

Ramon began college at Tel Aviv University in 1983. He was twenty-nine years old. He studied electronics and computer engineering. One night, Ramon went to a birthday party for a friend. He met a woman at the party named Rona Bar Simantov. They fell in love and were married just six months later. Ramon graduated from Tel Aviv University in 1987. He worked for Israel Aircraft Industries for a little while developing a new kind of fighter jet.

In 1988, Ramon went back to the military life he loved. He said, "I decided to go back to the air force, mainly because of the people that you work with there. They're really the best—devoted, friendly, and highly educated. I think the surroundings that you work in are very important, and I decided I'd be better off in the air force, where there were challenges that excited me." That same year brought another exciting change in Ramon's life. He and his wife, Rona, had their first child. They had a son and named him Assaf.

For the next two years, Ramon served as a deputy squadron commander. He worked hard and took a squadron commanders course. He then served as a squadron commander from 1990 to 1992. By this time he had flown thousands of hours in fighter planes.

Ramon was an excellent pilot and a strong leader. The IAF made him a colonel in 1994. He was put in charge of the IAF's department of weapons development. Ramon was proud of this position. "I was in charge of the weapons systems for the entire air force and had to prioritize what to develop and what to purchase, from airplanes to weapons systems, missiles, guns, computers, radars, communications—everything," he said. Ramon kept this job for four years. Then he got a phone call in April 1997 that changed his life forever.

In August 1994, Ramon was presented with the rank of colonel in the Israeli Air Force by Ehud Barak, then the Israeli chief of staff. Ramon's wife, Rona, helps him add his new epaulets to his uniform.

Israel's First Astronaut

A few years earlier, former U.S. president Bill Clinton and Israeli prime minister Shimon Peres had a meeting. They agreed that Israel would choose someone to train as an astronaut in the U.S. space program. He or she would carry out scientific experiments on a future space-shuttle mission. The person chosen would become Israel's first astronaut. That person needed to be part of the Israeli Air Force, have an education in science, and have experience doing scientific work with the IAF.

The competition was very tough. But Ramon's track record made him a top pick. Lieutenant Colonel Oded Bar Ziv was a former squadron commander with Ramon. He said, "When he [Ramon] was picked to be the first astronaut, no one was surprised. He was the natural choice." But Ramon was very surprised!

When Ramon got that special phone call he thought a co-worker was playing a joke on him. Then it started to sink in. "They came and tapped me on the shoulder and asked me if I wanted to be an astronaut," he said later. "It came completely out of the blue. Of course, I did not refuse." Ramon drove home slowly that night. He was thinking about what life as an astronaut might be like.

Training to be an astronaut is a full-time job, but Ramon took time off for a summer vacation with his wife, Rona, and the kids, from left, Assaf, Yiftah, Noa, and Tal.

Ilan and Rona had three more children by that time. Two more boys—Tal and Yiftah—and a little girl named Noa. Ramon wasn't the only one about to begin a new adventure. Their entire family of six left Israel and moved to Houston, Texas, in 1998. None of Ramon's children spoke any English except Assaf. But they all started public school when they got to Texas. They joined a synagogue, made new friends, and learned English. The Ramon family began to get used to their new lives in America. Ramon began training at NASA's Johnson Space Center (JSC).

What Is a Space Shuttle?

Columbia was the oldest shuttle in NASA's space-shuttle program. It made its first flight on April 12, 1981. Four more spacecraft were built to join the program over the next ten years.

NASA started the space-shuttle program in the 1960s. Shuttles are used to launch and pick up satellites, transport people and things to the *International Space Station* (ISS), and conduct experiments in space. Before there were space shuttles, the rockets that were sent into space could only be used once. But shuttles are designed to come back to Earth. They are launched like rockets and land like airplanes. A space shuttle has three main parts: the orbiter, the external fuel tank, and the rocket boosters. The orbiter points upward like a rocket when a shuttle is being prepared for launch. The fuel tank and rocket boosters are attached to the orbiter. The boosters give the orbiter the extra power it needs to be lifted off the launchpad.

The shuttle is launched, clears the tower, and climbs upward. The rocket boosters burn for only two minutes before separating from the external tank. They drop into the Atlantic Ocean with the help of a parachute. (They are picked up by a ship so they can be used for another mission.)

Several minutes later, the external fuel tank separates from the orbiter. As it falls, it burns up in the atmosphere. Without the boosters and the external tank, the orbiter looks much like an airplane as it heads into space.

The astronauts aboard the shuttle live in the crew compartment. This is where they eat, drink, sleep, and exercise. It is also where they control the shuttle and run experiments. Extra laboratory space is included for research on some missions. The orbiter has everything the astronauts need to live comfortably while in space.

The orbiter prepares for landing after the mission is complete and it is time to return to Earth. It gets into the right position and slows down. Temperatures are very hot when the shuttle re-enters Earth's atmosphere. The orbiter is covered with materials that keep it cool. This protects the shuttle and the astronauts inside. When all goes as planned, the shuttle safely enters the main atmosphere of Earth. Then it makes its way to the landing strip. The shuttle program has been very successful. It has made dozens of safe trips into space over the years.

As launch day approaches, Ramon, Anderson, and Clark suit up and practice the launch sequence.

The next four years were busy for Ramon. He took classes such as shuttle systems, navigation, astronomy, physics, and survival training. There are three different positions for astronauts aboard a shuttle—commander/pilots, mission specialists, and payload specialists. Payload specialists have special duties such as being in charge of specific scientific experiments. This was Ramon's job on *Columbia*. He trained hard as an astronaut. He also spent a lot of time learning about and preparing for the experiments he would run aboard the shuttle.

In America, most of the news about a new shuttle mission begins to be reported close to the date of liftoff. But in Israel, the news ran frequent stories about Ramon starting from the time he was chosen to be part of the space-shuttle crew. The Israelis followed the progress of their first astronaut step-by-step. The year 2002 was named "The Year of Space" in Israel. And a postage stamp was made in honor of his upcoming shuttle launch. It was easy to like Ramon. He was smart, brave, charming, warm, handsome, and humble. He made a perfect national hero.

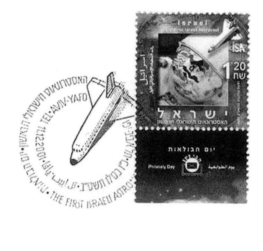

One of the things people wanted to hear about was the list of things Ramon planned to take with him into space. Astronauts usually take some personal things with them when they leave their families behind on a mission. These items, such as photographs, music, and letters, help them feel connected to home. Ramon's wife, Rona, sent Ilan into space with four poems. His son Assaf gave him a letter to read while he was in orbit. Ramon's brother, Gadi, did the same. And his father, Eliezer, gave him a few family photographs. Ramon also decided to bring some Jewish symbols into space with him.

Astronaut Jobs

Astronauts have many different jobs to handle in order to keep the shuttle on course and the mission on track. Duties are shared among three different types of astronaut positions aboard the shuttle. These positions are commander/pilots, mission specialists, and payload specialists.

Commander/pilots serve as both pilots and commanders. The commander is in charge of the overall safety and success of the mission. A commander/pilot helps the commander fly the shuttle. The pilot also operates the shuttle's robotic arm if picking up a satellite is part of the mission.

Mission specialists are responsible for making sure all the shuttle systems are running smoothly and that the goals of a mission are being carried out. They organize the activity of the crew and are in charge of all the technical support of running scientific experiments on board the shuttle. They also handle many of the actual experiments of a mission.

In order to become a commander/pilot or mission specialist, a person needs a college degree in engineering, math, biology, or physics. Mission specialists also need a graduate school degree and/or to have worked for three years in a related field. Pilots must have flown in command of jet aircraft for at least 1,000 hours, pass a tough physical exam, and be between 64 and 76 inches tall.

The smallest number of crewmembers a shuttle can have is five. A payload specialist is added when a mission needs more than five crewmembers. They are often chosen to do a very specific job on board the shuttle that usually relates to scientific experiments. To be considered for the job, a person needs to have plenty of experience related to the work he or she will do on the shuttle. A NASA physical must also be passed. Ilan Ramon was a payload specialist on board *Columbia*.

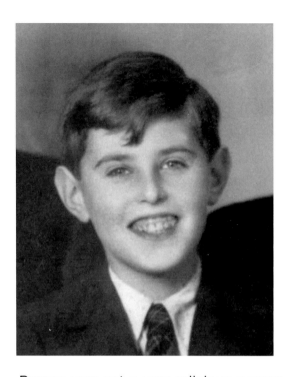

Ramon was not a very religious person. But he had begun to realize how important it was to be the first Israeli to travel into space. "Every time you are the first, it is meaningful. I am told my flight is meaningful to a lot of Jewish people around the world. Being the first Israeli astronaut, I feel I am representing all Jews and all Israelis." Because of this, and because his mother lived through the Holocaust, Ramon chose a few things he felt had special meaning.

One was a copy of a drawing that a fourteen-year-old boy did nearly sixty years ago. Petr Ginz died during World War II in Auschwitz. This was the same concentration camp where Ramon's mother had been. Petr's pencil drawing touched Ramon. It is called *Moon Landscape*. It shows Petr's vision of what Earth would look like from the Moon.

Ramon learned more about Petr. He discovered that the boy loved drawing, reading, and science. He also found out that the survivors of Petr's family had ended up in the same Israeli town—Beersheba—as Ramon's family. Ramon talked about taking the drawing with him into space. "I feel that my journey fulfills the dream of Petr Ginz fifty-eight years on." Ramon believed Petr's drawing was a symbol of how strong a person's spirit can be even in terrible times.

Ramon also carried a mezuzah with him into space. A mezuzah is a small piece of parchment with a passage from the Torah, the Hebrew Bible, on it. This parchment is rolled up and put in a small decorative container. A mezuzah is often hung in the doorway of a Jewish home. An artist named Aimee Golant made the one Ramon took with him. Her grandparents were survivors of the Holocaust.

Artist Aimee Golant holds another of her "barbed wire" mezuzahs. The barbed wire represents the time of the Holocaust, when so many Jewish people were held in camps behind barbed wire. The Star of David, in the center, is a symbol of Israel.

Opposite page, right: Petr Ginz's drawing, a copy of which went to space with Ilan Ramon. Left: This photograph of Petr Ginz was taken in happier times, before World War II started.

23

The third thing Ramon took aboard *Columbia* was a small Torah scroll. This scroll made an incredible journey and had its own story to tell. It was given to a young boy by a rabbi.

The boy's name was Joachim Joseph. He was thirteen years old in March 1944. He was in a German concentration camp called Bergen-Belsen. It was time for his bar mitzvah. A bar mitzvah is the Jewish ceremony that marks the passage into adulthood. Of course, there was no synagogue in the concentration camp. But there was a rabbi in the same living quarters as Joseph. Rabbi Simon Dasberg took out a tiny Torah he had managed to keep with him. The windows were covered so the Nazi guards could not see what they were doing inside. Joseph and Rabbi Dasberg read from the Torah and performed his bar mitzvah. Rabbi Dasberg then gave Joseph the Torah. He said, "You take this, this scroll that you just read from, because I will not leave here alive. But you must promise me that if you get out, you'll tell the story."

Joachim Joseph traveled from Israel to the NASA Goddard Space Center in Maryland to receive the data that his friend Ilan Ramon would be sending back from space.

Ramon, with the flags of both Israel and the United States proudly worn on his uniform.

Joseph did get out, and he did have a chance to tell the story. He told it to his friend Ramon almost sixty years later. Ramon saw the Torah scroll while visiting Joseph's house in Israel. The two men were working on a project together. Joseph was one of the Israeli scientists from Tel Aviv University in charge of an experiment Ramon was doing aboard the *Columbia*. Ramon later called Joseph from Texas and asked if he could take the Torah into space with him. Joseph was thrilled.

After the shuttle tragedy Joseph said, "I am not sorry that it didn't come back. Ilan allowed me to fulfill my promise to Rabbi Dasberg. I would never have been able to reach the whole world without Ilan. I think the Torah scroll did its job on earth and in space."

To represent his country, Ramon also wore a patch of the Israeli flag on his space suit. Israel has a long history of trouble involving its borders. Ramon hoped his efforts might play a small part in helping people see things from a different point of view. "When we go up to space, Earth is one unity and no borders are seen from there. That's the vision that NASA carries on and that is my vision too," he said.

Food in Space

What do astronauts eat in space? At first, in the early days of space flights, space food wasn't too exciting.

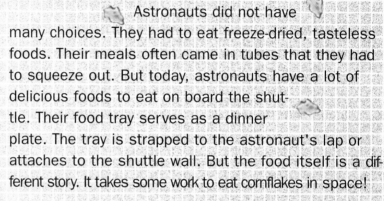

Astronauts did not have many choices. They had to eat freeze-dried, tasteless foods. Their meals often came in tubes that they had to squeeze out. But today, astronauts have a lot of delicious foods to eat on board the shuttle. Their food tray serves as a dinner plate. The tray is strapped to the astronaut's lap or attaches to the shuttle wall. But the food itself is a different story. It takes some work to eat cornflakes in space!

NASA is careful to make sure the astronauts get balanced meals with enough calories to keep them going. Many of the foods are similar to ones found in any grocery store. Astronauts can even help plan their own menus. When Ilan Ramon set out to plan his meals he asked NASA if he could have some kosher food. He said, "Personally, I don't keep kosher and my family doesn't follow all the religious rules, but since I feel I represent all kinds of Israeli people and the Jewish community, I thought it would be nice if I could have kosher food."

NASA agreed and helped Ramon with his request. Ramon enjoyed kosher Old World Stew, Chicken with Noodles, and Chicken

Mediterranean on board the shuttle. In addition to the kosher food he asked for, Ramon also ate tortillas, scrambled eggs, green beans, trail mix, and brownies.

Some teachers may frown on students trading food at lunch. But space-shuttle astronauts love to try one another's choices. That's because being in space can change how things taste. They may also just want to try something new to spice things up! Some members of *Columbia* wanted to sample kosher food. Ramon said, "My crewmates share with me and love it."

Liftoff!

Columbia was ready to be launched into space on January 16, 2003. It was the first shuttle trip in three years that was mostly for scientific research. Other recent trips focused on traveling to the *International Space Station* (ISS) or repairing the Hubble Space Telescope.

Hundreds of people gathered in Cape Canaveral, Florida, to watch the launch. Ramon's wife and children were there. After the launch a reporter asked Rona how she felt watching her husband's shuttle take off. "I'm so happy. I know he is laughing all the way up. Because he is doing exactly what he wants to do," she said. Ramon's son Assaf said, "I wanted to be a fighter pilot because I grew up with it and was surrounded by it. It looks like a lot of fun. And my dad did it. He's one of the best guys, so that inspired me. Now I want to go to space like my dad."

The launch was shown live in the United States and Israel. People stopped what they were doing as the countdown began. The only sound heard in a busy Jerusalem restaurant was that of people counting along.

The faces of Israel's technology minister, Limor Livnat, left, and the prime minister, Ariel Sharon, reflect their joy and delight at speaking with Ramon in space. Ramon and fellow astronauts William McCool and Laurel Clark are being seen by the prime minister on television screens around the room.

Ramon's father was one of the millions watching the launch in Israel. "My heart is beating very fast. This is the moment I was waiting for," he said just minutes after seeing the launch on television.

The daily news in Israel is often filled with reports of violence because of the constant border struggles there. But on January 16 one newscaster opened with, "Finally we can begin with good news." Ramon's journey into space was cause for major celebration. Israeli television reporter Yonit Levy was excited. She said, "Ilan Ramon is taking his place in the history books. One of the sons of the State of Israel will gaze at us from space." Ramon reached new heights of fame and glory as he made his way skyward.

Science in Space

During this mission, a total of eighty experiments were planned. The space-shuttle crew worked on a variety of biology, chemistry, physics, and climate experiments. The astronauts went into action just hours after liftoff. The first thing to do was activate the SpaceHab module, the laboratory space on board. They opened the hatch leading into SpaceHab, checked on the animals aboard, and turned on lights, cameras, and recording equipment. Ramon radioed in, "We're ready to go."

The crew worked twenty-four hours a day while they were in space. They formed two teams–red and blue–and took turns sleeping. During a live broadcast from space, Ramon told a group of ninth graders about one of his favorite parts of life aboard the shuttle. He said, ". . . the floating, going to sleep in a little closet and floating inside it is something like the magicians show us. It really is tremendous."

One of the main experiments Ramon ran is called the Mediterranean Israeli Dust Experiment (MEIDEX). Ramon kept a careful watch for dust clouds. He aimed the MEIDEX camera at them whenever he saw one.

SpaceHab is connected to the shuttle by a tunnel the astronauts must climb through to work on the many experiments aboard.

The camera measured the dust particles in the atmosphere. Tracking the flow of dust helps scientists better understand changes in Earth's atmosphere, climate, and weather. It also helps them see how viruses move through the air.

Students ready their experiments to be loaded on SpaceHab.

Joachim Joseph, whose Torah went into space with Ramon, is a scientist working on the MEIDEX at Tel Aviv University. "It's important to know where the dust is and what it is doing. Dust acts against the effect of greenhouse gases. Desert dust is also an important source of minerals for ocean life. It transfers spores, bacteria, and viruses such as influenza from continent to continent," Joseph explained. MEIDEX also found unusual electrical activity in thunderstorms. Ramon sent most of the data from MEIDEX to Joseph before the shuttle was destroyed.

Ramon also worked on an experiment to see how flames create soot. He set tiny fires in a special container. Scientists hope to learn how to cut down on pollution by learning why some soot is dirtier than others. Another one of Ramon's projects looked at how weightlessness affects the growth of bone cells. And along with his crew members, Ramon studied the effects of space on his own body. He wore a watch with a tiny computer in it that kept track of things like his activity during sleep, his heartbeat, and other bodily functions.

A program called Space Technology and Research Students (STARS) allows kids to get involved with space science, too. Students all over the world can submit their experiment ideas to STARS. If their idea is chosen, they move on to planning the details of their experiment. Ramon worked on STARS projects and reported back to the students from space. In a NASA interview about the program he said, "What is exciting about STARS is that the students are the one[s] who had the idea, planned the experiment, planned how it worked, participate in putting the hardware together, and of course analyze it post flight. So, it's really exciting." Kimberly Campbell, a manager of the STARS program, said about Ramon, "He got very involved in STARS and actually asked to be assigned to the STARS program to work with students' experiments worldwide."

Floating in the shuttle, Ramon is clearly enjoying the ride.

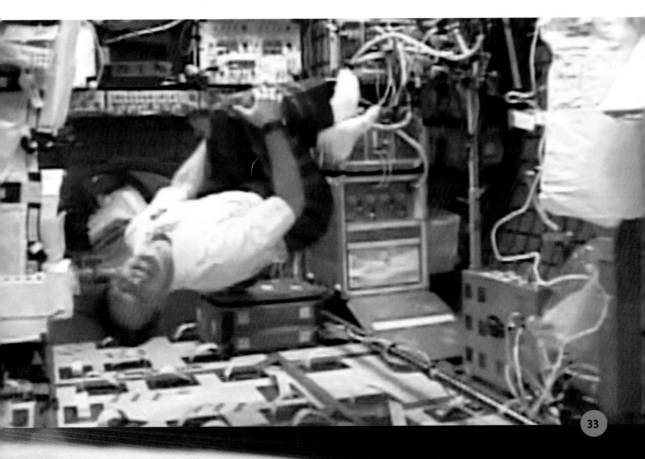

Through STARS, kids from six different countries had the chance to create experiments that flew aboard *Columbia*. Australian students wanted to see how a spider would spin a web in space. Chinese students sent silkworms into orbit. Children from Liechtenstein sent bees to be observed on board the shuttle. And Japanese students designed an experiment to see if a certain type of fish egg would develop more quickly in space.

American high school students from New York State were interested in learning if ants make tunnels differently in space. They sent an ant farm up with the astronauts. Data sent back from the shuttle during the mission showed surprising results. The students thought the ants would tunnel more slowly in space. Instead, student Abby Golash said, "They ended up tunneling like maniacs."

Opposite: Ramon with the experiment known as the chemical garden. Israeli students expected that crystals would grow by building on themselves in a straight line, like they do on Earth. Instead, Ramon reported to the students that the crystals grew every which way, as if they were crystal roots.
Above: Ramon and mission specialist Kalpana Chawla in SpaceHab.

A group of students from Israel designed an experiment for Ramon to run. They wanted to learn how the lack of gravity in space affects the growth of crystals. The crystals were blue cobalt and white calcium—the two colors of the Israeli flag. They called their project the chemical garden. On January 24, 2003, Ramon gave an update on the STARS projects from the shuttle. "On the silkworm from China we noticed one [cocoon] that actually hatched and we have a butterfly in there. . . . The bees and the ants and the spider are alive, and the chemical garden is blooming."

The Israeli eighth graders who sent up the chemical garden had gathered at a friend's house to watch the shuttle land. In shock and despair, they saw the shuttle disaster on television.

The students cried with the rest of the world when the shuttle was lost. Ramon had spent some time at the Israeli school talking with the kids about their work. A student named Dor Zafrir said, "He approached each and every one of us, asked us how we feel, what we think. You could feel his genuine interest." Students from Syracuse, New York, had never met the *Columbia* crew. But they were closely linked through the work they shared. "We felt part of the space program," Brad Miller said. "We all felt like a little piece of us was gone when the shuttle disappeared." Miller and his classmates decided to continue their research to honor the astronauts.

Fallen Heroes

Astronauts know the risk they are taking when they journey into space. But that doesn't make losing them any easier when tragedy strikes. All over the world, people mourned the fallen astronauts. In Israel, headlines read "Crying for Ilan" and "Pieces of the Dream." People lit candles, made signs, played sad music, and held memorials in honor of the first Israeli astronaut—Ilan Ramon.

Ramon was busy with the hard work of the *Columbia* mission while he was in space. But he also took time to see the magic of where he was. He talked about how beautiful the Earth is and how the human race needs to care for it. "The world looks marvelous from up here, so peaceful, so wonderful and so fragile. The atmosphere is so thin and fragile, and I think all of us have to keep it clean and good. It saves our life and gives our life." He also spoke about his homeland as he flew over Israel. Ramon said, "The quiet that envelops space makes the beauty even more powerful, and I only hope that the quiet can one day spread to my country."

Above: Ilan Ramon watches the horizon of the Earth through the small window of a darkened shuttle.
Opposite: An honor guard carries the coffin of Ilan Ramon to a plane that will carry him home to Israel.

Ramon is remembered as many things—an astronaut, a role model, a father, a husband, a brother, a son, and a friend. Ramon's friend Joachim Joseph said, ". . . I think Ilan represented the good part in each and every one of us. He was a true Israeli hero—brave, straightforward and optimistic. He was a good role model for us." Joseph also remembered Ramon as "active and quick and intelligent, caring, so it was impossible not to like him. He was just that kind of guy. When you saw him, you immediately took to him. I particularly liked the way he interacted with his children."

All of Ramon's children were close to their father. A friend of the family remembered how Ilan made time for his kids no matter how busy he was at work. When his children called him at NASA, he always found the time to talk with them. He even went to summer camp with his son Yiftah last year to speak with the campers about his life as an astronaut.

While in space, Ramon was often on the minds of his children and their friends. Taylor Heeke, a classmate of his son Tal, said a group of kids was walking together one day and started waving and shouting hello as if they could see Ramon in the sky. She said, "Tal just stood there laughing at us. We talked about his dad all the time. He was really excited about his father going in space, and he was really proud of him, too."

Ramon's funeral was held at Lod Air Force Base in Israel on February 11, 2003. A fellow pilot and friend of Ramon's played a song on the saxophone. It was the same song Ramon's wife, Rona, had played for Ilan while he was aboard *Columbia*. The words are "You will hear my voice calling you from far away." Rona and their four children sat with Israeli prime minister Ariel Sharon. Ramon's oldest son, fifteen-year-old Assaf, proudly wore his father's blue-and-white NASA jacket. Their five-year-old daughter, Noa, sat in her mother's lap for comfort.

During the service Sharon said, "This is not how how we imagined you coming home. Ilan touched a hidden spot in the soul of every Jew. He brought something out in us . . . his youthful face, his constant smile, that wonderful light in his eyes—all of this has gone straight to our hearts. He went higher than anyone else and made his dream come true."

Rona seemed to find some peace in the idea that her husband died doing what he loved best. She told a television reporter, "We take comfort that Ilan left [us] at his peak moment in his favorite place, with people he loved." She said about her husband, "He wasn't afraid. He left us with a feeling of confidence . . . everyone who knows him, knows that it's impossible to remember him without a smile on his face, and we will continue forward with that same smile."

Chronology

June 20, 1954	Ilan Wolferman (Ramon) is born near Tel Aviv, Israel.
1970	Takes his first ride in a small plane
1972	Graduates from high school
	Enters the Israeli Air Force (IAF)
1973	Serves in the Yom Kippur War
1974	Graduates from flight school
1980	Trains to fly F-16s in Utah, United States
1982	Serves in Operation Peace for Galilee
1983	Enters Tel Aviv University
1986	Marries Rona Bar Simantov
1987	Graduates from Tel Aviv University
1988	Rejoins the Israeli Air Force
1994	Is promoted to colonel and put in charge of weapons development
1997	Is asked to become Israel's first astronaut
1998	Family moves to Texas
January 16, 2003	*Columbia* lifts off.
February 1, 2003	*Columbia* is lost.

Sources

Abbey, Alan D. "Ilan Ramon–Israeli Hero." *Internet Jerusalem Post*, February 1, 2003.

Ben-Tal, Daniel, and Tovah Lazaroff. "Ilan Ramon Laid to Rest." *Internet Jerusalem Post*, February 12, 2003.

Bernstein, Alan, and Bennett Roth. "Prayers for the Fallen: Symbols, Personal Remembrances Highlight Memorial." *Houston Chronicle*, February 5, 2003.

Brown, Irene. "After Delays, Israeli Fighter Pilot Poised to Soar into Space With NASA." JTA, December 22, 2002.

Cabbage, Michael. "Ilan Ramon." *Orlando Sentinel*, February 2003.

————. "Israeli Astronaut to Carry Culture, Nation's Hopes on Shuttle." *Orlando Sentinel*, February 1, 2003.

Carreau, Mark. "Israeli Star Flies High; Nation's Astronaut to Open Door to Space." *Houston Chronicle*, January 15, 2003.

————. "Shuttle Lifts Off Amid Tight Security." *Houston Chronicle*, January 17, 2003.

Chien, Philip. "A Personal Look at *Columbia's* Crew." *Internet Jerusalem Post*, February 9, 2003.

————. "Ilan Ramon Talks About His Experience in Space." *Internet Jerusalem Post*, January 19, 2003.

————. "Ilan Ramon Tends Student Experiments." *Internet Jerusalem Post*, January 25, 2003.

————. "Life in Space for Ilan Ramon." *Internet Jerusalem Post*, February 3, 2003.

————. "Ramon Fired Up About Experiments." *Internet Jerusalem Post*, January 19, 2003.

Ephron, Dan. "An Outpouring of Grief Spreads Through Israel." *Houston Chronicle,* February 2, 2003.

"Farewell *Columbia*." Staff article, *People*, February 17, 2003.

Farrell, Stephen. "Nation Mourns Pilot Who Reached for the Stars." *Times Newspapers, Ltd.*, February 3, 2003.

Gelfond, Lauren. "Sister of Concentration Camp Artist Remembers Drawing Ramon Took With Him." *Internet Jerusalem Post*, February 4, 2003.

Greenberg, Joel. "Israelis Enjoy Sense of Pride, History With First Hebrew Astronaut." Chicago Tribune, January 16, 2003.

————. "Israel Mourns Countryman Lost to Heavens." *Chicago Tribune*, February 2, 2003.

Harel, Amos. "Ramon's First Combat Mission: Iraq." *Haaretz English Edition Online*, March 2, 2003.

Healy, Patrick. "Israel Remembers Its Fallen Astronaut." *Boston Globe*, February 11, 2003.

Herel, Suzanne. "Israeli Took Mezuzah Into Space." *San Francisco Chronicle*, February 2, 2003.

Keinon, Herb. "Astronaut Lifts Nation's Spirits." *Internet Jerusalem Post*, January 22, 2003.

Kluger, Jeffrey. "What Went Wrong?" *Time Magazine*, February 10, 2003.

Kramer, Lauren. "The Sky Is Not the Limit." *Lifestyles*, Issue 169, Fall 2000.

Lazaroff, Tovah. "We'll Remember Him With a Smile on His Face." *Internet Jerusalem Post*, February 3, 2003.

—————. "A Promise Fulfilled." *Internet Jerusalem Post*, February 19, 2003.

Leary, Warren E. "Profile: Ilan Ramon." *The New York Times*, February 2, 2003.

—————. "Col. Ilan Ramon: Pilot Embraced Role as a Symbol for Jews." *The New York Times*, February 1, 2003.

"The Magnificent Seven." 2003 Special Commemorative Issue, *U.S. News & World Report*. Section on Ilan Ramon written by Larry Derfner and Samantha Levine, February 2003.

Markley, Melanie. "Schools Teach, Learn Lessons From Tragedy." *Houston Chronicle*, February 4, 2003.

McGran, Kevin. "Israeli Pilot Was 'Something Special.'" *Toronto Star*, February 2, 2003.

"My Heart Is Beating Very Fast." Staff article. *Internet Jerusalem Post*, January 16, 2003.

Myre, Greg. "Israel Grieves Over Death of First Astronaut." Associated Press, February 1, 2003.

"School Ant Experiment to Honor Astronauts." Associated Press, reported on CNN, February 4, 2003.

Smith, Wes. "Houston Feels Personal Loss." *Orlando Sentinel*. February 2, 2003.

Wilgoren, Debbi. "The Torah That Went From the Depths to the Heavens." *The Washington Post*, February 19, 2003.

Wilgoren, Debbi, and Molly Moore. "For National Hero, Space Was a Natural Step." *The Washington Post*, February 10, 2003.

Wohlgelernter, Elli. "Holocaust Helped Define Ramon's Identity." *Internet Jerusalem Post*, February 2, 2003.

Internet Addresses

For an absolutely amazing, interactive view of the components of a space shuttle and how it is launched, visit How Stuff Works at:

http://www.howstuffworks.com/space-shuttle.htm/printable

To learn how students are able to participate in designing experiments for future missions, visit the Space Technology and Research Students (STARS) program online at:
http://www.starsacademy.com/sts107/

Have you ever wanted to go to space camp? Visit this site to learn more. Go to:

http://www.spacecamp.com/welcome.asp

NASA has lots of great things to read and see on their Web site, http://spaceflight.nasa.gov

To see an interactive listing of past shuttle launches, visit:

http://spaceflight.nasa.gov/shuttle/archives/index.html

To see an interactive listing of future shuttle launches, visit:

http://spaceflight.nasa.gov/shuttle/future/index.html

To go behind the scenes and find out about all the planning that goes into a space-shuttle mission, visit:

http://spaceflight.nasa.gov/shuttle/support/index.html

Have you got what it takes to become an astronaut? Learn how one person prepared for her astronaut job.

http://spaceflight.nasa.gov/outreach/jobsinfo/astronaut.html

Index

Courtesy of Bonnie Christensen

About the Author

Tanya Lee Stone is a former editor of children's books who now writes full-time. She has a Masters Degree in Science Education.

Tanya is the author of more than 50 books for kids, including *Laura Welch Bush: First Lady; Blastoff! Mars; Blastoff! Saturn; The Great Depression and World War II; Living in a World of Green: Where Survival Means Blending In; Lizards; Kangaroos; Lions; Koalas; D is for Dreidel: A Hanukkah Alphabet Book; and M is for Mistletoe: A Christmas Alphabet Book.*

She lives in Burlington, Vermont, with her husband Alan and their two wonderful children. You are invited to visit her on the web at www.tanyastone.com.